a story to tell

DEVOTIONS FOR LENT
2021

AUGSBURG FORTRESS

Minneapolis

A STORY TO TELL
Devotions for Lent 2021

pISBN 978-1-5064-6949-2
eISBN 978-1-5064-7433-5

Writers: Bekki Lohrmann (February 17–27), Harvard Stephens Jr. (February 28–March 11), Lydia Posselt (March 12–22), David L. Miller (March 23–April 3)

Editor: Laurie J. Hanson
Cover image: Path through the Magic Forest iStock/SrdjanPav
Cover design: Alisha Lofgren
Interior design: Eileen Engebretson
Interior photos: All images © iStock. Used by permission.

20   21   1   2   3   4   5

Welcome

A Story to Tell provides daily devotions for each day from Ash Wednesday to the Vigil of Easter (traditionally known as Holy Saturday). Devotions begin with an evocative image and a brief passage from the Gospel of Mark (the gospel focus for 2021, year B in the Revised Common Lectionary). The writers then bring their unique voices and pastoral wisdom to the Mark texts with quotations to ponder, reflections, and prayers.

The Gospel of Mark has a story to tell about "the good news of Jesus Christ, the Son of God" (1:1). This story is told quickly and urgently, as if there's no time to spare. Yet the most reliable manuscripts for Mark's gospel end with women running in fear from the empty tomb, telling no one what they have seen and heard (16:8).

May this Lenten journey through Mark's gospel strengthen and inspire you to tell the story of Jesus Christ through all you do and say.

Listen, listen, God is calling, through the Word inviting, offering forgiveness, comfort, and joy.
Jesus gave his mandate: share the good news
that he came to save us and set us free.
—"Listen, God Is Calling/*Neno lake Mungu*," ELW 513, refrain, st. 1

February 17 / Ash Wednesday

Mark 1:1-3

The beginning of the good news of Jesus Christ, the Son of God.
As it is written in the prophet Isaiah,
"See, I am sending my messenger ahead of you,
who will prepare your way;
the voice of one crying out in the wilderness:
'Prepare the way of the Lord, make his paths straight.'"

To ponder

Ignatius of Loyola chose a word for this purity of intention—
indifference—and used that word in a particular way. By it, he
meant being as free as is humanly possible to follow the call of
God.—Elizabeth Liebert, *The Way of Discernment*

Start by shedding

How do your beginnings go? How do you usually get started on something? Do you plan or procrastinate? Are you cautious or do you just jump right in? How is your Lenten journey beginning today?

The Gospel of Mark begins with a call to prepare, but this preparation looks different than the kind we're used to. Often our preparations involve loading up—packing for a trip, shopping back-to-school sales, or cramming for a test, but this is not the sort of preparation the gospel calls us to today. Instead this preparation looks a lot like shedding—shedding what we think we know, confessing our shortcomings, and owning up to what we have and haven't done. We shed and shed until we are capable of wild indifference (which is different from apathy), releasing our personal agendas and letting go of hoped-for outcomes until we feel quite bare. There in that stripped-down state, with empty hands, we are ready and open to receive Christ.

Prayer

God, take what you must from me until I am unburdened and therefore ready to receive what you have for me. Amen.

Mark 1:4-8

John the baptizer appeared in the wilderness, proclaiming a baptism of repentance for the forgiveness of sins. And people from the whole Judean countryside and all the people of Jerusalem were going out to him, and were baptized by him in the river Jordan, confessing their sins. Now John was clothed with camel's hair, with a leather belt around his waist, and he ate locusts and wild honey. He proclaimed, "The one who is more powerful than I is coming after me; I am not worthy to stoop down and untie the thong of his sandals. I have baptized you with water; but he will baptize you with the Holy Spirit."

To ponder

Child of God, you have been sealed by the Holy Spirit and marked with the cross of Christ forever.—*Evangelical Lutheran Worship*, Holy Baptism

Baptized with the Spirit

Centuries ago it was common practice to seal letters by pressing something, such as the emblem on a ring, into a small circle of warm wax. The impression made in the wax authenticated the letter's origin. When a letter had the seal of the king, you knew it came from the king.

All who are baptized bear God's seal. Our human lives are like warm wax—malleable, moldable, and impressionable. And the wild yet gentle, creative yet unchanging, tranquil yet agitating Spirit of God impresses upon us so that our shape, our style, and the specific curvature of our being is the authentication of where we came from. We bear the image of God in everything from our bones to our breath. Take a moment and breathe in that truth, giving thanks for your Spirit-infused, enlivened existence.

Prayer

Triune God, whose image I bear, give me the clarity and the courage to accept the specific shape of my own existence—the parts I deem ugly, the rough-shod places, the beautiful parts, and everything in between—because in the intricate contours of my life, the impression of your seal is to be found. Amen.

Mark 1:9-11

In those days Jesus came from Nazareth of Galilee and was baptized by John in the Jordan. And just as he was coming up out of the water, he saw the heavens torn apart and the Spirit descending like a dove on him. And a voice came from heaven, "You are my Son, the Beloved; with you I am well pleased."

To ponder

Baptism is a renunciation of all those competing voices that try and tell you who you are. The world . . . gives you names like screw-up, faker, fat . . . in baptism you're named "Beloved."
—Rachel Held Evans, "Named Beloved"

Call me "beloved"

Think about Jesus, born in a barn in first-century Palestine to a woman who became pregnant before she was married. The name *illegitimate* could have ordered his existence, every day challenging his legitimacy.

King Herod ordered the killing of young children in and around Bethlehem as he attempted to get rid of the child sought by the magi. The name *troublemaker* could have followed Jesus, every day living with his head down to never challenge the status quo.

Angels sang at Jesus' birth; a star appeared in the sky; wise men came bearing expensive gifts; random people at the temple praised him. He could have spent his life marked by the name *extraordinary*, every day expecting to be the center of the universe.

These names could have shaped Jesus' life, but they all fell away when God named him *Beloved*. We too receive this name in baptism, and under it we can move free, with nothing to prove, every day.

Prayer

Beloved Jesus, thank you for giving me your name, for pouring it out over me freely and for all time. Amen.

Mark 1:12-15

And the Spirit immediately drove him out into the wilderness. He was in the wilderness forty days, tempted by Satan; and he was with the wild beasts; and the angels waited on him.

Now after John was arrested, Jesus came to Galilee, proclaiming the good news of God, and saying, "The time is fulfilled, and the kingdom of God has come near; repent, and believe in the good news."

To ponder

The voice of shame in our heads—that is the Accuser. The accusing voice telling me that I am what I've done or that what I *am* is wrong. . . . When that accusing voice is on repeat in your head, know that it is not the voice of God. God's voice is found in the warm singsong of a mother to her newborn, the one who says, "You are beloved." . . . This is the use of the Christian community, as I see it. We help each other silence the Accuser.—Nadia Bolz-Weber, *Shameless*

Silencing shame

Living without a name for the entity that shames us is like living with an undiagnosed disease. Day after day you feel awful but don't know it's related to an illness. You start thinking there is no hope for you. Then at your yearly physical, you learn you have symptoms of a disease that has a name. Suddenly you can see yourself apart from the symptoms and begin to treat the disease.

When the Accuser's voice begins to wrap around you, constricting your movement and making the space around and within you dismal and desolate, shaming you into thinking you are worthless and unlovable, know that it has a name and that the church is here to shut down that loudmouth.

Prayer

Loving God, I'm repeatedly tempted to trust the Accuser's lies over your truth. Protect me from this temptation, and anchor me today in the truth of your love and forgiveness, in Jesus' name. Amen.

February 21 / Lent 1

Mark 1:19-20

[Jesus] saw James son of Zebedee and his brother John, who were in their boat mending the nets. Immediately he called them; and they left their father Zebedee in the boat with the hired men, and followed him.

To ponder

It is the fate of human beings to exist in-between the world as it is and the world as it should be. . . . When these two worlds collide hard enough and often enough, a fire in the belly is sometimes ignited. The tension between the two worlds is the root of radical action for justice.—Edward T. Chambers, *Roots for Radicals*

From one world into another

In commercial fishing you're looking for the best fish—big, juicy, meaty fish. That's where the money is. This is like the world we live in—a world of seeking out the best and using that to make a profit, using tools that need mending and constant upkeep. We live in this grind.

Jesus calls us out of the world as it is. At the sound of his voice, we dare to let go, relinquishing the systems we cling to for power, the mechanisms we have created to accumulate wealth, the nets we have strung up to make it through our day but that leave others tangled and struggling to live. In Christ, we see it all for what it is and drop it along with our old nets.

Jesus meets us in the world as we know it and calls us into the world as it could be—a world where we fish not for the healthiest, biggest, or brawniest, but for the sick, tossed-aside, and undesirable. We fish not for profit, but to do the work of accompaniment that allows all to flourish.

Prayer

Ever-present Christ, give us the courage to work in the space between the world as it is and the world as it will be under the reign of your love. Amen.

Mark 1:21, 23-26

When the sabbath came, [Jesus] entered the synagogue and taught.... Just then there was in their synagogue a man with an unclean spirit, and he cried out, "What have you to do with us, Jesus of Nazareth? Have you come to destroy us? I know who you are, the Holy One of God." But Jesus rebuked him, saying, "Be silent, and come out of him!" And the unclean spirit, convulsing him and crying with a loud voice, came out of him.

To ponder

I just know that demons, whether they be addictions or evil spirits, are not what Jesus wants for us.—Nadia Bolz-Weber, "Demon Possession"

Show up

Jesus isn't one who hides or dips his toe in to take the temperature of the moment before deciding how he will respond to a situation. He's always all in, all Jesus, all the time, no matter who likes it or doesn't like it. On several occasions his "all-in-ness" results in attacks from demons.

Demons do not want us to show up all in like Jesus. They are their most contrary when we show up no-holds-barred. They bully, belittle, and berate to get us to follow their lead and to be less than ourselves. But it is not our fate to follow demons down their rabbit holes. We have been given the same authority as Jesus. The next time a bullying word or thought comes to you, flick it away. God's desire is for you to show up all in, all the way, as you share Christ's love in the world.

Prayer

Jesus, you never let demons bully you. Put your power behind my tongue, that every time I am assailed into thinking I ought to be less than myself, I can say no, in Jesus' name. Amen.

February 23

Mark 2:3-5

Some people came, bringing to [Jesus] a paralyzed man, carried by four of them. And when they could not bring him to Jesus because of the crowd, they removed the roof above [Jesus]; and after having dug through it, they let down the mat on which the paralytic lay. When Jesus saw their faith, he said to the paralytic, "Son, your sins are forgiven."

To ponder

Jesus is in a house so packed that no one can come through the door anymore. . . . The focus of the story is, understandably, the healing of the paralytic. But there is something more significant than that happening here. They're ripping the roof off the place, and those outside are being let in.—Greg Boyle, *Tattoos on the Heart*

A time to tear down

Think about what it takes to knead dough. The hand works the outer edge of the dough into the center. As what was the center of the dough becomes the outer edge, the hand folds it back in. This is our work as followers of Christ—to bring those who are on the outside to the center again and again.

In most cases that work doesn't happen as seamlessly as kneading dough, however. A barrier—a policy (or lack of one), an ideology, a wall, a roof—often prevents what is on the outside from moving to the inside. Whatever the barrier is, it keeps the outsider out.

In serving at the soup kitchen, working at the food bank, giving away warm blankets and quilts, and much more, the church goes out to meet people where they are. This is an important part of God's healing work in the world. Another part of God's healing work is to tear down structures that leave folks on the outside in the first place. It's messy work but in that torn-up house we meet Christ.

Prayer

God our healer, move us and mobilize us to tear the roof off a world where people have been shut out, in Jesus' name. Amen.

Mark 2:6-8

Now some of the scribes were sitting there, questioning in their hearts, "Why does this fellow speak in this way? It is blasphemy! Who can forgive sins but God alone?" At once Jesus perceived in his spirit that they were discussing these questions among themselves; and he said to them, "Why do you raise such questions in your hearts?"

To ponder

Jesus heals but in healing shows us how sick we are. Jesus forgives but in forgiving shows us how sinful we are. Jesus teaches good news but in teaching shows us how much we don't know. And it can be painful to see and hear these things.—Benjamin J. Dueholm, "Hearing the Truth"

Beyond being nice

Jesus regularly found himself in a position of opposition, which is good news to folks wearied by the simplistic notion that Christians are nice people. That "nice" image can restrict us to the point that all we can do is sit on our hands. We are caring, loving, and generous; and caring, loving, generous people don't go around upsetting other people with their actions! Do you see how this image can bind us and restrict our movement?

We do not follow images of what it is to be Christian, however. We follow Christ, who had no difficulty showing compassion even when others found it offensive, loving all people despite the way that agitated others, being bold and humble all at once. Likewise we are called upon to love in ways that offend—by reaching out to someone who believes differently than we do, protesting injustice, setting a boundary, challenging an assumption, forgiving an enemy. It won't always feel good, but feeling good is not the aim. The aim is faithfulness, which can be messy.

Prayer

Despised Christ, when it's called for, give me courage to do the loving thing that's going to upset the apple cart. Amen.

February 25

Mark 2:9-12

[Jesus said,] "Which is easier, to say to the paralytic, 'Your sins are forgiven,' or to say, 'Stand up and take your mat and walk'? But so that you may know that the Son of Man has authority on earth to forgive sins"—he said to the paralytic—"I say to you, stand up, take your mat and go to your home." And he stood up, and immediately took the mat and went out before all of them; so that they were all amazed and glorified God, saying, "We have never seen anything like this!"

To ponder

It's this strange experience of being let go by someone that enables you to let go of yourself and come to be something bigger than you thought you were, realizing that it's someone else who made that possible for you. That's what I mean by being forgiven.

—James Alison, "The Forgiving Victim"

Please just let me pick up my mat and walk

I don't know which is easier to *say*, "Your sins are forgiven" or "Stand up and walk." But I know which is easier to *hear*: "Stand up, take your mat, and walk." In this command I have something I can do, an action I can take. I get to claim some agency for the fact that I'm no longer down and out.

When Jesus says, "Your sins are forgiven," I am completely vulnerable to his verdict. To make matters worse, to be forgiven means that I did something that needed forgiveness. It's excruciating to be seen for what I am in that way. Because we don't like feeling powerless, we sometimes reject the one forgiving us. But in doing that we forfeit the gift that makes us into something bigger than we ever knew we could be.

Prayer

God, I'd rather be my own god, picking up my own broken life and walking away on my own. But if that were the case, I'd be down forever. Thank you for your forgiveness, which enables me to get up and carry on, in Jesus' name. Amen.

February 26

Mark 2:14-16

As [Jesus] was walking along, he saw Levi son of Alphaeus sitting at the tax booth, and he said to him, "Follow me." And he got up and followed him. And as he sat at dinner in Levi's house . . . the scribes of the Pharisees . . . said to his disciples, "Why does he eat with tax collectors and sinners?"

To ponder

It is God's intent that the stones that were once seen as unfit to be a part of the architecture, the stones that were once thrown away or kept in the quarry, have now been called to be the chief cornerstones. . . . Whenever you see rejected stones and rejected people becoming the focus of society, it is the Lord's doing.—William J. Barber II, sermon at Disciples of Christ General Assembly

No accounting for taste

What is God calling you to be? You might think, "God isn't calling me into God's service. I'm not kind enough, humble enough, good enough. In fact, I'm a huge liability!" Here's the thing—you might be right about being a liability.

Levi the tax collector was a liability. His presence attracted the scrutiny of the Pharisees and scribes, which eventually got Jesus killed. Then again, maybe Levi's presence wasn't a liability—maybe that was the point! Maybe Levi was called to follow, not to *advance* Jesus' cause, but because he *was* Jesus' cause.

Before you discredit yourself today for being too x, y, or z, remember that God has a long history of choosing to love and call folks in a way that makes no logical sense to us. Our lives move to the beat of a God who loves in God's own way, with no accounting for taste!

Prayer

Jesus, you chose to dine with the likes of Levi, so I'm going to stop trying to figure out why you want me in your company and just accept that you have strange taste. I couldn't be more grateful for that. Amen.

Mark 3:1-5

[Jesus] entered the synagogue, and a man was there who had a withered hand. [The Pharisees] watched him to see whether he would cure him on the sabbath, so that they might accuse him. . . . Then he said to them, "Is it lawful to do good or to do harm on the sabbath, to save life or to kill?" But they were silent. He looked around at them with anger; he was grieved at their hardness of heart and said to the man, "Stretch out your hand." He stretched it out, and his hand was restored.

To ponder

This is why it's so hard to have a real conversation, because people don't trust each other's motives; they think the other person is

motivated by something bad, while they are motivated by something good. And the only way we really get to dispel that is when we build true authentic relationship with each other and that can only happen when we're willing to open up and be vulnerable.
—Vivek Murthy, "Dr. Vivek Murthy and Brené on Loneliness and Connection"

What we think we know

What's going on here with the Pharisees is tragic. There is a man with a withered hand, and perhaps a withered existence, and there is Jesus, who has come to restore what is withered to fullness. But the Pharisees come to the synagogue with an agenda that precludes them from seeing the events unfolding right in front of them. The text says they watched "so that they might accuse him." This is what hardness of heart looks like—being so fixed on an outcome that we miss what God is doing right under our noses, and miss the kingdom of God coming near.

What outcomes, agendas, or biases are preventing you from seeing God's restoration work happening right beneath your nose?

Prayer

Christ our healer, we're a clingy lot, holding fast to what we think we know. Come, Lord Jesus, soften our hearts so we can see signs of your salvation, healing, and life around us. Amen.

February 28 / Lent 2

Mark 4:3-8

[Jesus said,] "Listen! A sower went out to sow. And as he sowed, some seed fell on the path, and the birds came and ate it up. Other seed fell on rocky ground. . . . And when the sun rose, it was scorched; and since it had no root, it withered away. Other seed fell among thorns, and the thorns grew up and choked it, and it yielded no grain. Other seed fell into good soil and brought forth grain, growing up and increasing and yielding thirty and sixty and a hundredfold."

To ponder

We plant the seeds that one day will grow. We water seeds already planted, knowing that they hold future promise. . . . We cannot do

everything, and there is a sense of liberation in realizing that. . . .
It may be incomplete, but it is a beginning, a step along the way,
an opportunity for the Lord's grace to enter and do the rest.
—Ken Untener, "Prophets of a Future Not Our Own"

God gives the growth

People familiar with farming or gardening know that seeds
planted in the soil take time to sprout. They do not become
anxious while nature takes its course; they trust that at the right
time seeds will grow.

This is also how the reign of God unfolds. We long to see
many of the same things that faithful leaders and martyrs before
us struggled to fashion: a world that values faith, truth, justice,
and kindness. God calls us to do our part in announcing God's
promises. We give thanks for the ways the kingdom of God
appears in the world we inhabit, but also pray for those who will
come after us to gather a harvest from the seeds we have sown.

Prayer

Holy God, creator of hopes and dreams, let your will be done
in us and through us. Free us from anxiety and distress as we
struggle to accept the limits of our strength and power. Renew
our trust in your promises to make known the wonders of your
new creation. Amen.

March 1

Mark 4:30-32

[Jesus] also said, "With what can we compare the kingdom of God, or what parable will we use for it? It is like a mustard seed, which, when sown upon the ground, is the smallest of all the seeds on earth; yet when it is sown it grows up and becomes the greatest of all shrubs, and puts forth large branches, so that the birds of the air can make nests in its shade."

To ponder

There is no end to the things that can awaken our wonder, from the majesty of the night sky, to the smell of lilacs in the spring, to the turning of the leaves in the fall . . . a feast of epiphanies and astonishments in the daily round of our lives.—Frederic and Mary Ann Brussat, *Spiritual Rx*

Surprises ahead

Jesus speaks in awe of the kingdom of God, an extraordinary mystery. From a small and insignificant seed grows a magnificent shrub that provides shade for flocks of birds. This image is not about science or horticulture; it is a profound celebration of the ways God's divine presence can be revealed in our lives. The mustard seed can even reflect the wonders of our own spiritual gifts.

Stories of God's reign remind us that many surprises await us as we live faithfully in the love of Christ. Who helps you recognize the miracles of amazing grace that persistently appear in your life, even in seasons of struggle and doubt? Rejoice in the company of those who faithfully admire God's unceasing wonders.

Prayer

God of wonder, God of might, draw near and reveal to us the majesty of the little things you fill with holiness and grace. As we recognize what you are doing to heal, save, and restore this broken world, teach us to rejoice in the miracles of your love. Amen.

March 2

Mark 5:22-24

Then one of the leaders of the synagogue named Jairus came and, when he saw [Jesus], fell at his feet and begged him repeatedly, "My little daughter is at the point of death. Come and lay your hands on her, so that she may be made well, and live." So he went with him.

To ponder

We have to learn how to take people in again or the poverty and the political hatred and the decimation of peoples and the turning of our own lives into icy islands will never end. . . . Real hospitality for our time requires that, instead of flipping the channel or turning the page, we try to determine what it is about our own lives that is affecting these others.—Joan Chittister, *Wisdom Distilled from the Daily*

Making room in our hearts

The devastations caused by COVID-19 have spared no individual, no community, no nation. Responses to the pandemic have included fear, anger, selfishness, and impatience, as well as generosity, kindness, and compassion. Some have acted rashly, taking risks that endanger the lives of others. Others have risked their own health to provide care for those who are sick and suffering.

When synagogue leader Jairus reached out to Jesus in desperation, Jesus responded by simply going with him. Jesus calls us to make room in our hearts to be present with others and to assist our neighbors across the street and around the globe, as God's transforming love works through our hearts and hands and voices.

Prayer

Loving Jesus, bring healing and hope to our lives, to the church, and to the world. Take away our fears and prejudices as you open our hearts to the needs of others. Amen.

March 3

Mark 5:25, 27-29, 34

Now there was a woman who had been suffering from hemorrhages for twelve years.... She had heard about Jesus, and came up behind him in the crowd and touched his cloak, for she said, "If I but touch his clothes, I will be made well." Immediately her hemorrhage stopped; and she felt in her body that she was healed of her disease.... [Jesus] said to her, "Daughter, your faith has made you well; go in peace, and be healed of your disease."

To ponder

Timidly we get off the train.... We board our first Yankee street car to go to a cousin's home.... We have been told that we can sit where we please, but we are still scared. We cannot shake off three hundred years of fear in three hours.—Richard Wright, *12 Million Black Voices*

Free at last

People live among us with untold stories of severe hardships they have endured. However brief or extended the span of time, these powerful stories expose forces still at work to cause suffering, discouragement, and despair.

A timid walk up the aisle of a church, a fearful ride on a formerly segregated streetcar, an uncertain response to Jesus' probing question "Who touched me?"—all reveal the lingering fear of rejection. Going against expectations established by indifference and injustice is difficult. Jesus, however, lifts up those the world wants to keep down. We have new stories to tell, surprising stories about the transforming power of Jesus' love to overcome the ways of this world. These powerful stories of faith truly make us whole.

Prayer

Holy One, we are humbled by your passion to confront the forces that demean and diminish us. Thank you for stories of faith that show the power of your redeeming love. Bless us with hope that is greater than fear and despair. Amen.

March 4

Mark 5:35-36, 40-43

Some people came from the leader's house to say, "Your daughter is dead. Why trouble the teacher any further?" But overhearing what they said, Jesus said to the leader of the synagogue, "Do not fear, only believe." . . . [Jesus] went in where the child was. He took her by the hand and said to her, "Talitha cum," which means, "Little girl, get up!" And immediately the girl got up and began to walk about. . . . He strictly ordered them that no one should know this, and told them to give her something to eat.

To ponder

Ask the precocious first grader marching out of Vacation Bible School with a Jesus-themed coloring book under her arm and she will likely say, "The good news is Jesus loves me, this I know, for the Bible tells me so." And she will be right. . . . The gospel means that every small story is part of a sweeping story, every ordinary life part of an extraordinary movement. God is busy making all things new.—Rachel Held Evans, *Inspired*

Taste and see

The season of Lent anticipates a great feast and joyful baptisms in honor of the resurrection of our Lord. As we journey together these forty days, our hunger grows for all that awaits us. Along the way in these devotions, we hear stories from Jesus' life and ministry—stories meant for sharing, stories that are part of the larger story of how God makes all things new.

In today's story of healing, the father's faithful persistence, rather than his social standing as a leader of the synagogue, brings Jesus to the girl's side to save her. Now the room is filled with the aroma of food, the splashing of cleansing water, and other expressions of the family's profound gratitude.

Taste and see that the Lord is good.

Prayer

Compassionate Lord, take our hands, touch our hearts, feed us, and inspire us to lift our voices in prayer, praise, and witness to the story of your love for us and all creation. Amen.

March 5

Mark 6:35-38

When it grew late, [Jesus'] disciples came to him and said, "This is a deserted place, and the hour is now very late; send [the crowd] away so that they may go into the surrounding country and villages and buy something for themselves to eat." But he answered them, "You give them something to eat." They said to him, "Are we to go and buy two hundred denarii worth of bread, and give it to them to eat?" And he said to them, "How many loaves have you? Go and see." When they had found out, they said, "Five, and two fish."

To ponder

When we live our lives strictly in private, concerned only with our own consumption, when we hoard and do not share, then we live in continual fear of scarcity and never learn of the riches that a public life can bring.—Parker J. Palmer, *The Company of Strangers*

Teach us to share

Five loaves of bread and two fish were all the food the disciples could find to feed the crowd. That initial meager fare is a stark reminder that when no preparations are made for travel through a deserted place, the outcome can be brutal.

In today's world, the term *food deserts* describes places that have little access to fresh food at a fair price. Far too often, people living in these places suffer from the poor health that accompanies a poor diet. Many urban food deserts exist in reasonable proximity to an abundance of food, but political and social barriers keep those who are poor from obtaining what they need.

Jesus noticed that people in the crowd were hungry, and challenged his disciples to meet this need. He continues to challenge his disciples today, and calls us into a new community where all are fed. Feeding others is part of who we are as his body, his church, and indeed, his people.

Prayer

We look to you, O God, to care for our bodies and souls. Awaken us to do our part to end the scourge of hunger. Amen.

March 6

Mark 6:39, 41-43

Then [Jesus] ordered [the disciples] to get all the people to sit down in groups on the green grass.... Taking the five loaves and the two fish, he looked up to heaven, and blessed and broke the loaves, and gave them to his disciples to set before the people; and he divided the two fish among them all. And all ate and were filled; and they took up twelve baskets full of broken pieces and of the fish.

To ponder

Work needn't be suffering; it could unite folks.... A mother [could] raise her daughter with love and kindness. A beautiful soul like Caesar could be anything he wanted here.... In her

Georgia misery she had pictured freedom, and it had not looked like this. Freedom was a community laboring for something lovely and rare.—Colson Whitehead, *The Underground Railroad*

Something lovely and rare

This miraculous feeding of more than five thousand people is a magnificent story of a new community coming together. As Jesus directs this hungry assembly to sit down in groups, marvel at the inclusiveness of these clusters of people about to be fed. Jesus calls them to eat together and to experience the rich ritual of passing food from hand to hand. The former strangers are now bound together because of what the Lord has done for them. They become a cloud of witnesses who share a common story of abundant blessings poured out through the compassion of Christ. This is something lovely and rare indeed.

Our ministries bring light to the world as we create and sustain new communities that exude signs of God's amazing grace. A new community, a new creation, a new heart, a new commandment—these are made possible by Jesus' redeeming love. Baptized into his name, we have been liberated, set free to discover again and again the astounding wonders of God's love and blessings.

Prayer

Come, Lord Jesus, our holy guest. Your gifts to us are always blessed. Amen.

March 7 / Lent 3

Mark 7:32-35

They brought to [Jesus] a deaf man who had an impediment in his speech; and they begged him to lay his hand on him. He took him aside in private, away from the crowd, and put his fingers into his ears, and he spat and touched his tongue. Then looking up to heaven, he sighed and said to him, "Ephphatha," that is, "Be opened." And immediately his ears were opened, his tongue was released, and he spoke plainly.

To ponder

Those who have been healed can be recognized by the fact that they can praise God. Those who are healed begin to sing; they stand up; they can hand on God's power themselves. Their eyes become capable of recognizing God's power in the people beside them. . . . All at once they can see where the kingdom of God has already begun.—Dorothee Soelle and Luise Schottroff, *Jesus of Nazareth*

Be opened

A seminary student with a hearing impairment pushed her community to be more inclusive of leaders like her. She pointed out that when the prayers of intercession were said in worship, she felt excluded by the words "Lord, in your mercy, hear our prayer." She proposed an alternative way to conclude the prayer petitions: "Lord, in your mercy, *receive* our prayer."

In today's Bible text, Jesus meets with a man privately and cries out, "Be opened." The man is healed, and the gifts of speaking and hearing with clarity and confidence open up to him.

Where is God calling for more openness in our lives, in the church, and in the world?

Prayer

Mighty Savior, open our hearts and minds to your love and your call to serve. Fill our senses with joy as your kingdom appears among us. Amen.

March 8

Mark 8:22-26

Some people brought a blind man to [Jesus] and begged him to touch him. . . . When [Jesus] had put saliva on his eyes and laid his hands on him, he asked him, "Can you see anything?" And the man looked up and said, "I can see people, but they look like trees, walking." Then Jesus laid his hands on his eyes again; and he looked intently and his sight was restored, and he saw everything clearly. Then he sent him away to his home, saying, "Do not even go into the village."

To ponder

Scholars have identified risk-taking spiritual types as "seekers" . . . individuals on a journey . . . beyond the faith traditions they inherited into new religious territory. . . . What if the story is not just the journey of a single blind girl? . . . What if those wanderers in the wilderness joined together? What if the whole village went on a journey to see?—Diana Butler Bass, *Christianity for the Rest of Us*

Do you see what I see?

Jesus healed this man and then told him not to go into the village. Was this to prevent skeptics from undermining the joy the man was surely feeling? We don't know. Jesus sent the man home instead, where family members and other companions were likely to join him in celebrating the astounding gift of healing.

How wonderful it is to experience the transforming work of God's grace in our lives, and to share this with people who will welcome, nurture, and support our life in Christ. We all need to find that person, that place that provides this kind of life-giving kinship. Don't let a village full of doubters and naysayers keep you from finding companions who will walk beside you on the journey to see and know the wonders of the Holy One.

Prayer

Thank you, Lord Jesus, for the great mysteries of your amazing grace. In all things, be our vision, our path, and our goal. Amen.

Mark 8:27-30

Jesus went on with his disciples to the villages of Caesarea Philippi; and on the way he asked his disciples, "Who do people say that I am?" And they answered him, "John the Baptist; and others, Elijah; and still others, one of the prophets." He asked them, "But who do you say that I am?" Peter answered him, "You are the Messiah." And he sternly ordered them not to tell anyone about him.

To ponder

One day, a close friend said to me, "No one can beat you being you. You have something unique to offer in your preaching and ministry that no one else can give. The people who come to hear you preach come because they want to hear you and what you have to share, the way you share it."—Cynthia L. Hale, in *More Power in the Pulpit*

I love to tell the story

Don't turn this conversation between Jesus and Peter into a nondisclosure agreement. The drama and tensions that fill the scriptures are intended to help us understand Jesus and his disciples in a variety of ways. In the gospels Peter is a leader whose actions don't always match his bold words. In the book of Acts he becomes a strong witness to Christ.

Who do you say that Jesus is? Even without speaking a word, you reveal your answer to this question, in ways that are unique to you. You communicate Jesus' message of grace, redeeming love, healing, justice, and peace by what you do as well as by what you say. Rejoice in knowing that God has entrusted the gospel to you—and to me.

Prayer

Giver of good news, thank you for the unique ways you equip me to tell the story of Jesus and his love. Thanks be to God. Amen.

March 10

Mark 8:31-33

[Jesus] began to teach them that the Son of Man must undergo great suffering, and be rejected by the elders, the chief priests, and the scribes, and be killed, and after three days rise again. . . . And Peter took him aside and began to rebuke him. But turning and looking at his disciples, he rebuked Peter and said, "Get behind me, Satan! For you are setting your mind not on divine things but on human things."

To ponder

In God's promise and call we find a new identity—an identity that frees us to be able to risk our very lives, because we have a secure future. . . . We don't know quite where we're going. . . .

God never promises that the path will be straight, direct, or easy. It leads through the valley of the shadow of death, but as the psalmist says, we don't travel alone.—Dwight J. Zscheile, *The Agile Church*

What we know about the future

Our plans are never one hundred percent certain. What we strive to create or accomplish is easily undone by unexpected events and circumstances. Few of us had imagined a pandemic that would bring death and economic disruption on such a global scale. Plans have been changed, canceled, postponed, and completely undone by COVID-19

Peter had plans for Jesus the Messiah that did not include suffering and dying on a cross. Given all that Peter had seen Jesus accomplish, he couldn't imagine his remarkable ministry ending in such a way. Jesus, however, spoke with quiet confidence about rising again after three days.

God did raise Jesus from death and is at work still today to bring life out of death and hope out of despair. As we move forward into each new day, Christ's loving presence will never leave us.

Prayer

God of truth, fill us with hope as you heal and renew us and the world. Amen.

March 11

Mark 8:34-36

[Jesus said,] "If any want to become my followers, let them deny themselves and take up their cross and follow me. For those who want to save their life will lose it, and those who lose their life for my sake, and for the sake of the gospel, will save it. For what will it profit them to gain the whole world and forfeit their life?"

To ponder

It is easy enough to claim belief in God. But the question that must always be put to such claims is, simply, Which God? What is your image of this God in whom you claim belief? What kind of company does your God keep? What does your God ask of you—if anything?—Douglas John Hall, *The Cross in Our Context*

There is a cross for me

A popular entertainer sings about losing yourself in moments that must be embraced even when they involve great risks. These lyrics remind me of Jesus' words: "Let them deny themselves and take up their cross and follow me."

In denying ourselves we put the needs of others ahead of our own self-interest and success. Crosses are signs of what we are called to do, however difficult or improbable, as Jesus leads the way. Many people have found peace, honor, and purpose in denying themselves, taking up the cross, and following Jesus. This does not conform to the logic of this world, but Christ's redeeming love gives us new life, strength, and wisdom that the world cannot give.

Prayer

Dear Jesus, encourage and sustain us as we take up the cross and follow you. Give us faith to go where you are leading us, trusting that, even amid suffering and death, you are the giver of life, joy, and peace. Amen.

March 12

Mark 9:2-5

Jesus took with him Peter and James and John, and led them up
a high mountain apart, by themselves. And he was transfigured
before them, and his clothes became dazzling white. . . . And there
appeared to them Elijah with Moses, who were talking with Jesus.
Then Peter said to Jesus, "Rabbi, it is good for us to be here; let
us make three dwellings, one for you, one for Moses, and one for
Elijah."

To ponder

I remember what I tell my students. "If it is God you want, look for
the light and not the diamond. There are so many facets, and yet

the light is not in any of them. Their beauty lies in the ability to reflect what is beyond them."—Barbara Brown Taylor, *Holy Envy*

Hinge moments

We often "go through our lives just going through our lives," as a friend reflected, until we experience a "hinge moment" or turning point that sets us on a new path. Sometimes these moments are unexpected—a shocking diagnosis, a surprising job opportunity, a near-miss while driving, an accidental meeting, a pandemic. Other hinge moments take months or even years of preparation—a wedding, a birth, a graduation, a baptism. But we can't wear a wedding dress or cap and gown forever. In these moments when we may be both awed and terrified, we get stuck with Peter wanting to build a hut and stay where we are. It would be much easier and more comfortable to stay up there on the mountain.

This moment in Jesus' life is the hinge that pivots him from his baptism to his crucifixion. Jesus shines with the love of God that day on the mountain, but also in his teaching and preaching, healing, and death. We are meant to shine too, but not just in during the high points in our lives. It's good for us to be here on the mountain, but we are not supposed to pitch a tent and stay.

Prayer

Jesus, lead the way, light our path, and give us the courage to shine with your love. Amen.

March 13

Mark 9:7-8

Then a cloud overshadowed them, and from the cloud there came a voice, "This is my Son, the Beloved; listen to him!" Suddenly when they looked around, they saw no one with them any more, but only Jesus.

To ponder

He said, "Family is a prayer. Wife is a prayer. Marriage is a prayer."

"Baptism is a prayer."

"No," he said. "Baptism is what I'd call a fact." —Marilynne Robinson, *Lila*

Listen to the truth

In the Gospel of Mark, Jesus' story begins with his baptism, when the heavens are torn apart and a voice says, "You are my Son, the Beloved; with you I am well pleased" (1:11). Today we find ourselves right in the middle of Mark's story about Jesus, at a moment when Jesus is transformed before his disciples and reveals his true nature. Only this time, God includes an addendum: "Listen to him!"

With Jesus' words and actions, he says and shows that we are beloved children of God. When other voices attempt to convince us that we are only dim bulbs and sputtering wicks, the voice of Jesus tells us we have the light of God shining in us. When you are tempted to believe otherwise, listen to this truth: You are loved. You are valued. God created you, and God sees you. This is a fact, and nothing can ever change it. Our fear seems to become a little dimmer because of this fact. Together we can shine, to rival even the sun in the sky and beyond. So, as God says, listen up! Listen to Jesus. Get up, and do not be afraid.

Prayer

Precious Jesus, speak into our hearts, that we may speak truth into the lives of others. Amen.

March 14 / Lent 4

Mark 9:33-35

[Jesus and his disciples] came to Capernaum; and when he was in the house he asked them, "What were you arguing about on the way?" But they were silent, for on the way they had argued with one another who was the greatest. He sat down, called the twelve, and said to them, "Whoever wants to be first must be last of all and servant of all."

To ponder

We never stop belonging to each other. Our fates are always inexplicably tied to others—first by umbilicus, later by heartstrings.
—Hannah Shanks, *This Is My Body*

All in this together

As the coronavirus spread throughout the world, all sense of what is "normal" was thrown out the window. I began to cringe every time I saw or heard the phrase "the new normal." Slowly, as stay-at-home orders stretched on, we saw the nature of TV commercials change. First they celebrated real heroes caring for others' needs, but then ads morphed into saying, "We're all in this together—and buy this product."

I found myself purchasing an embarrassing amount of yoga pants. Granted, they were made from organic cotton from a small company, but did I really need four pairs? Perhaps not. I consoled myself that I was supporting a small business, as I focused most of my purchases at that time on keeping open those businesses that reflected my values—or at least values that I believe reflect the kingdom of God—including justice, equity, fair wages, and minimal harm to the planet. I could not be out there myself helping people in need, but perhaps in a small way I could serve the most vulnerable by staying out of the way of people making a real difference— people who put themselves "last" and served, cared for, and protected others. People like these are first in the kingdom of God.

Prayer

Jesus, servant of all, you humbled yourself to save us. Help us to follow your example. Amen.

Mark 10:13-14, 16

People were bringing little children to [Jesus] in order that he might touch them; and the disciples spoke sternly to them. But when Jesus saw this, he was indignant and said to them, "Let the little children come to me; do not stop them; for it is to such as these that the kingdom of God belongs." . . . And he took them up in his arms, laid his hands on them, and blessed them.

To ponder

I've often said that those who say having a childlike faith means not asking questions haven't met too many children.—Rachel Held Evans, *Inspired*

Red light, green light, cupcake

During our "youngest disciples' time" in a Lenten worship service, I talked about playing the game "Red Light, Green Light." Perhaps your rules are a little different, but many kids play it this way: A leader calls, "Red light," "Green light," or perhaps "Yellow light," and everyone else stops, runs forward, or moves forward in slow motion, respectively. The object is to reach the leader. The person who wins becomes the next leader.

At one point I asked the children, "What would you do if the leader called, 'Purple light'?" I hoped for some variation on yellow light— moving slowly and intentionally, taking time to reflect, as we do in Lent—and we did eventually get there. The first response, however, from five-year-old Daisy, was to "be a cupcake"—a classic children's sermon surprise answer! Give this girl an honorary theology degree, because she was right. In Lent we move "purple," which can mean "be a cupcake." Cupcakes aren't just miniature cakes. They are concentrated, bite-sized, portable treats that are easily personalized, and do not require silverware or even a plate (though maybe a napkin). In other words, cupcakes are exactly what baptized and beloved children of God should be in the world—transportable, adaptable, unique, miniature Christs.

Let's be cupcakes during this Lent. Pass the frosting.

Prayer

Sweet Jesus, bless us and make us vessels to spread your love to others. Amen.

March 16

Mark 10:17-20

A man ran up and knelt before [Jesus], and asked him, "Good Teacher, what must I do to inherit eternal life?" Jesus said to him, "Why do you call me good? No one is good but God alone. You know the commandments: 'You shall not murder; You shall not commit adultery; You shall not steal; You shall not bear false witness; You shall not defraud; Honor your father and mother.'" He said to him, "Teacher, I have kept all these since my youth."

To ponder

I thought then of catechism classes, about chanting the answer to a question, an answer that was "because he has said it and his word is true." I could not remember the question.—Chimamanda Ngozi Adichie, *Purple Hibiscus*

What do I need to do?

"What must I do to inherit eternal life?" this young man asks. We know what he means: "Have I done enough to get into heaven?" Most of us have wondered that. But it's interesting that he uses the word *inherit*. What do you do to earn an inheritance? The answer is simple—absolutely nothing. The only criterion is that you are yourself, the receiver, the person to whom your benefactor is leaving their legacy. So what then can we do to inherit eternal life? Nothing. It isn't a matter of what you *do*, but who you *are*.

The gift of eternal life is the inheritance we receive at baptism, as we are washed with water and with God's promises: God claims us as beloved children. We receive the mark of the Holy Spirit. We belong to God forever. Through Christ, God does all of this for us.

Prayer

Grant us peace, dear Lord, when we are tempted to try to earn your goodness and mercy. Amen.

March 17

Mark 10:21-22

Jesus, looking at [the man], loved him and said, "You lack one thing; go, sell what you own, and give the money to the poor, and you will have treasure in heaven; then come, follow me." When he heard this, he was shocked and went away grieving, for he had many possessions.

To ponder

We are called to be anchored, above all, to the ethics of the kingdom of God. And when worldly understandings of respectful behavior preserve the power of some by silencing others, we must question whether those worldly understandings match the ethics to which God calls us and which Christ embodies.—Layton Williams, *Holy Disunity*

Too much of a good thing

I once read a graphic-novel version of the Gospel of Mark, and my favorite illustration was one for this story. The rich man approaches Jesus, deeply bent over because he is literally weighed down by a ridiculous number of items piled high on his back: surf boards, bowling balls, a couch, a convertible. As Jesus talks to him, the man slowly sinks into the sand under the weight, until he completely disappears.

How much is enough? This story makes us nervous because we wonder if Jesus is speaking specifically to this man's situation as a potential follower, or to all potential followers (meaning us). Maybe both can be true at the same time. We hold onto things in case we might have use for them; we buy things to fill real and imagined needs. Our accumulation can prevent or hamper our efforts to care for one another. Having things is nice, but things do not give life. We forget that with Jesus, we will never experience lack. Instead we will experience abundance of life, love, grace, forgiveness, relationship, and community.

Prayer

Gracious Lord, empty our hands and open our hearts to serve one another. Amen.

March 18

Mark 10:32-34

[Jesus] took the twelve aside again and began to tell them what was to happen to him, saying, "See, we are going up to Jerusalem, and the Son of Man will be handed over to the chief priests and the scribes, and they will condemn him to death; then they will hand him over to the Gentiles; they will mock him, and spit upon him, and flog him, and kill him; and after three days he will rise again."

To ponder

A minor melody marks our cadence, yet you tune my ears for more than that. Resurrection is always the final number.

—Arianne Braithwaite Lehn, *Ash and Starlight*

The End.

"And they all lived happily ever after." "True love's kiss broke the curse." "Tiny Tim observed, 'God bless us, every one!' The End."

Every story contains settings, characters, conflict, dialogue, a beginning, and an ending. But the beginnings and endings are what we tend to remember about good books, good movies, good stories in general. And at the end of the very best stories, the ones that stay with us, all the messy and complicated plot points are woven together in one giant and satisfying resolution. Some stories are better when we know the ending, but most of the time, we say "No spoilers please!" to friends who have already seen the movie or read the book. We want to be surprised.

God has a story, and we are part of it. God loves us so much that God gave away the ending, to give us hope during the hard parts. We (and the disciples) are let in on the secret—life comes after death and joy comes after suffering. And in every chapter, Jesus walks the road ahead of us and with us, so that at every twist and turn we are never alone.

Prayer

Lord of life, preserve and protect us when struggles and disasters strike. Amen.

Mark 11:7-10

Then [the disciples] brought the colt to Jesus and threw their cloaks on it; and he sat on it. Many people spread their cloaks on the road, and others spread leafy branches that they had cut in the fields. Then those who went ahead and those who followed were shouting, "Hosanna! Blessed is the one who comes in the name of the Lord! Blessed is the coming kingdom of our ancestor David! Hosanna in the highest heaven!"

To ponder

Waking up can be a jarring experience. Think of the loud, clanging alarm clock that goes off while you are in dreamland. You come to with a jolt that rocks you and leaves your heart racing. It can be a struggle to get your bearings. You search for something or someone that grounds you. . . . And we all have a choice, either to hit the snooze button or to wake up.—Rozella Haydée White, *Love Big*

Out of joint

It all began with such high hopes. Jesus entered Jerusalem in a parade, leaves flying, people singing and shouting, and a donkey braying in protest. And it's no wonder there was a parade, for the people had seen some amazing things from Jesus in the last three years. He had healed people with skin diseases and people who had been paralyzed. He had calmed storms and cast out demons. He had fed thousands and told about God's amazing love for wayward people.

This is how Holy Week starts. It's a week when time doesn't behave properly, opening with a parade and ending with an execution. It's a time when a crowd shouts hosannas one minute and "Crucify him!" the next; when bread becomes Jesus' body and wine becomes his blood; when a criminal is pardoned and an innocent man dies; when a king is killed for not being the right kind of king; when disciples deny and run away scared, and women and soldiers stand witness at Jesus' death.

Prayer

Holy Jesus, may we witness your kingdom as it arrives in our lives. Amen.

Mark 11:15-17

Then [Jesus and the disciples] came to Jerusalem. And he entered the temple and began to drive out those who were selling and those who were buying in the temple, and he overturned the tables of the money changers and the seats of those who sold doves; and he would not allow anyone to carry anything through the temple. He was teaching and saying, "Is it not written, 'My house shall be called a house of prayer for all the nations'? But you have made it a den of robbers."

To ponder

Jesus's cleansing of the temple was not a sanctification of anger, his or mine, but it was a promise: anger in and of itself did not

make one unholy. Anger . . . could be a source for transformation, a reckoning where the most vulnerable had been least cared for.
—Emmy Kegler, *One Coin Found*

The currency of God

For millennia, coins have included images of rulers and those in power, suggesting that the person pictured on the coin enjoyed the special favor of heaven—or even was a god. The emperor of Rome was no different. His face and his name were seen and revered daily in the mundane task of buying and selling. The money in the temple in Jerusalem was stamped with the emperor's name and image.

But suddenly, thanks to Jesus, the tables are turned. Swindling the flock in the name of the divine would no longer be allowed in God's house. This was not a place to be filled with the image of Caesar but to be filled with people, who bear the image of God.

You are created in God's image, and in baptism you are named and claimed "child of God." You are favored, sought out by God.

Prayer

Loving Savior, grant us eyes to see your image in those who are vulnerable, and the holy anger to act against injustice. Amen.

March 21 / Lent 5

Mark 12:28-31

One of the scribes came near and heard them disputing with one another, and seeing that [Jesus] answered them well, he asked him, "Which commandment is the first of all?" Jesus answered, "The first is, 'Hear, O Israel: the Lord our God, the Lord is one; you shall love the Lord your God with all your heart, and with all your soul, and with all your mind, and with all your strength.' The second is this, 'You shall love your neighbor as yourself.' There is no other commandment greater than these."

To ponder

Grace is free. But loving the neighbor has a high cost.—Lenny Duncan, *Dear Church*

The love test

As usual, Jesus didn't quite stay in the parameters of the question posed to him. He did not reply with just one commandment, as the scribe had asked, but instead quoted two. Jesus knew the Torah and recognized that loving God is intimately tied to loving your neighbor. Trying to separate one from the other is a tricky business.

Jesus did not come to be human among us to give us more rules to follow, or to narrow down the rules to just the most important ones. Jesus did not come to give us the minimum requirement for getting into heaven. Loving the Lord our God with our entire hearts, souls, and minds, and loving our neighbor as ourselves, is not a lesson we memorize and recite to pass a test. Instead it is a lesson that takes a lifetime to learn, beginning the moment we are baptized and sent out to be hands and feet of Jesus, called to show God's love to the world.

Prayer

Jesus, teach us to love you with all that we are, and hasten our feet to meet and serve our neighbor. Amen.

March 22

Mark 12:41-44

[Jesus] sat down opposite the treasury, and watched the crowd putting money into the treasury. Many rich people put in large sums. A poor widow came and put in two small copper coins, which are worth a penny. Then he called his disciples and said to them, "Truly I tell you, this poor widow has put in more than all those who are contributing to the treasury. For all of them have contributed out of their abundance; but she out of her poverty has put in everything she had, all she had to live on."

To ponder

In God's economy, there is always enough.—Karen Gonzalez, *The God Who Sees*

Seen and valued

As Jesus watched, the wealthy made a show of writing big checks. Then a poor widow came, and in went the entire amount of what today might be her Social Security check. Jesus noticed that the rich had given what they could afford. The woman had given a larger proportion of what she had than any of them, even though she couldn't afford it.

In those days, a widow was at the mercy of others to survive. We don't know whether her children or extended family took care of this woman, or if she had a home. But we do know that her offering impressed Jesus more than all the vast sums the rich had contributed. Although she was invisible to society at large, and had no legal power or religious clout, she gave what little she did have. She was all in for God. She trusted that the God in whose image she was created, and to whom she belonged, would not forsake her. Whether she lived or died, she was seen. She had value. She belonged to God.

Prayer

Creator God, gift us with a spirit of generosity to share with trust and not hold back with fear. Amen.

March 23

Mark 14:3

While [Jesus] was at Bethany in the house of Simon the leper, as he sat at the table, a woman came with an alabaster jar of very costly ointment of nard, and she broke open the jar and poured the ointment on his head.

To ponder

Passion involves a transformation in which love of others, the desire to heal, to offer comfort and hope . . . take on a radically new character. When we allow authentic passion to have its way, we can return to love, and life, and service with new verve and feeling. The experience of passion wounds with the fire of love and opens the door to utter fullness of humanity in God.

—Elizabeth A. Dreyer, *Passionate Spirituality*

Only love

It is impossible for me not to love this unnamed woman, for her heart flows with the love I most want to feel. She grasps the handle of the jar in her right hand, her left caressing the stone curve of the body, balancing the weight. Without a word, she kneels beside Jesus and pours out the oil, her eyes never leaving the darkness of his hair. There is no one else in the world for her in this moment, just she and Jesus . . . and the lavish love spilling from her heart, more extravagant than the oil she pours. Why such love? What moves her to such excess?

Only love can do this, the love that wakes within when the soul is one with the heart of Christ. The silent passion in her eyes is a holy gift from the one who is God's love for us now and always. The very sight of her draws us to kneel there, beside Jesus, and share her work, hoping we might become as beautiful as she.

Prayer

Awaken holy passion in our hearts, O Lord, that, overwhelmed with love, we may give ourselves to you and be transformed in your likeness. Amen.

March 24

Mark 14:4-6, 8

But some were there who said to one another in anger, "Why was the ointment wasted in this way? For this ointment could have been sold . . . and the money given to the poor." And they scolded her. But Jesus said, "Let her alone; why do you trouble her? She has performed a good service for me. . . . She has done what she could; she has anointed my body beforehand for its burial."

To ponder

I don't want to end up simply having visited this world.—Mary Oliver, "When Death Comes"

Broken open

They're right, of course. The oil could have been sold and money given to the poor, and it would have been a good and noble thing to do. But mere logic can never grasp what the heart requires.

The woman's soul is so broken open in love that she pours it all out on Jesus, an anointing not of oil alone, but of the beauty he awakens in human hearts. Not counting the cost or considering what others think, she acts for the sake of love alone. The others did not yet understand, but chastised the self-giving that is the mark of those who fall in love with Jesus.

Perhaps the best question we might ask is, *Do we understand? Do we know the power of love moving us beyond ourselves and our fears to love beyond reason? Just what does love require of you?* Answer that question and you know exactly what Jesus is calling you to do.

Prayer

Break our hearts open, Lord Jesus, that we may pour ourselves out for this world you so love. Amen.

Mark 14:10-11

Then Judas Iscariot, who was one of the twelve, went to the chief priests in order to betray [Jesus] to them. When they heard it, they were greatly pleased, and promised to give him money. So he began to look for an opportunity to betray him.

To ponder

The Lord has redeemed all of us, all of us, with the Blood of Christ. . . . Everyone! "Father, the atheists?" Even the atheists. Everyone! And this Blood makes us children of God of the first class! We are created children in the likeness of God and the Blood of Christ has redeemed us all!—Pope Francis, "Pope at Mass"

Crooked lines

History hasn't been kind to Judas. His name is synonymous with betrayal for turning against the one truly good soul we've ever known. What did he want and what was he thinking as he snuck around, looking for the right moment to hand Jesus over to his enemies? Some evidence suggests he was dishonest and greedy, selling out for a few filthy bucks. Scholars suggest he became disenchanted, disappointed that Jesus hadn't started a revolution to usher in a new world. Maybe Judas thought he was lighting a fuse to ignite the conflict that would make Jesus king.

The older I get, the more likely I am to cut Judas a bit of slack, knowing my own mixed motives. I mean, when are our hearts utterly pure, untainted by self-interest? The good news is that ultimately even this doesn't matter, because God works with crooked lines—even with crooked people. Whatever Judas's motives, or ours, God doesn't hesitate using even our foulest acts to get what the divine heart wants—life, forgiveness, and blessing, even for confused and conflicted people. Pity Judas didn't stick around long enough to see that there was still room in God's great heart for him.

Prayer

Gracious God, use the best and the worst of what we do to accomplish your loving purpose. Amen.

March 26

Mark 14:13-15

[Jesus] sent two of his disciples, saying to them, "Go into the city, and a man carrying a jar of water will meet you; follow him, and wherever he enters, say to the owner of the house, 'The Teacher asks, Where is my guest room where I may eat the Passover with my disciples?' He will show you a large room upstairs."

To ponder

God's intention in creating the universe, it seems, is to create a place where all human beings could live as brothers and sisters in a community of faith, hope and love, united by God's Holy Spirit with Jesus Christ . . . in harmony with the whole created universe—William A. Barry, *Paying Attention to God*

Our story

No, no, this room is much too small. And those chairs, chilly and stiff, don't you think? We need something bigger, warmer. That's what I would have said about the room in today's picture, were I one of those two disciples. Fortunately, they found something more spacious and hospitable, and it's a good thing they did. Contrary to common depictions, there likely were more than twelve followers with Jesus at the last supper, and they probably reclined on cushions, no chairs needed.

Those two disciples went to find the room fit for Passover, a holy meal that tells a story of deliverance and hope. Passover recounts how God freed the people of Israel from bondage. Each person at the meal participates as the story is told so that they know, *This is my story. My life is part of the great story of God's liberating love.*

Jesus was about to write one more chapter in that story, surrendering his life to reveal the fullness of God's death-killing love and forgiveness for everyone—even for those who put him to death.

So he needed a big room, spacious and warm, for a story and a love that no room can hold.

Prayer

Move our hearts to sing the story of your love, O Lord, and to proclaim your faithfulness forever. Amen.

Mark 14:22-24

While they were eating, [Jesus] took a loaf of bread, and after blessing it he broke it, gave it to them, and said, "Take; this is my body." Then he took a cup, and after giving thanks he gave it to them, and all of them drank from it. He said to them, "This is my blood of the covenant, which is poured out for many."

To ponder

What, do you wish to know your Lord's meaning in this thing? Know it well, love was his meaning. Who reveals it to you? Love. What did he reveal to you? Love. Why does he reveal it to you? For love. Remain in this, and you will know more of the same. . .

Before God made us he loved us, which love was never abated and never will be.—Julian of Norwich, *Showings*

Hold out your hands

I wonder, Jesus, did you look at your hands and pause as you broke the loaf? Did a thousand memories race through your mind as you cracked the crust? Did a wave of emotion flood your heart as you remembered the aching eyes of those you touched and healed? Did tears sting your eyes as you turned to the confused faces of your friends?

I love you for this moment, for I see how human you are, how much like me and yet so much more. Here, one more time, you give yourself to those you love more than they will ever understand, longing for those whom you chose and taught, scolded, and loved in spite of themselves, hoping they will receive the unspeakable gift you offer.

Bread and wine, yes, perfect elements to share your divine heart—bread to fill the emptiness; wine to swoon the heart with awareness of boundless love. You hold back nothing, Jesus. You give everything you are, all of it, to those you love more than words can say, aching for them to hold out their hands.

Just . . . hold out your hands.

Prayer

Grant us the holy privilege of feeling the depth of your heart, Lord Jesus. Amen.

March 28 / Sunday of the Passion

Mark 14:32, 44-46

[Jesus and the disciples] went to a place called Gethsemane. . . .
Now the betrayer had given them a sign, saying, "The one I will
kiss is the man; arrest him and lead him away under guard." So
when he came, he went up to [Jesus] at once and said, "Rabbi!"
and kissed him. Then they laid hands on him and arrested him.

To ponder

Those hands . . . have protected me in times of danger and
consoled me in times of grief. They have waved good-bye and
always welcomed me back. Those hands are God's hands. They

are also the hands of my parents, teachers, friends, healers, and all those whom God has given me to remind me how safely I am held.—Henri J. M. Nouwen, *The Return of the Prodigal Son*

Those hands

I remember Grant Ronnerud's hands, sun-bleached, fingers thick as a half dollar, chapped by sun and wind, strong from carrying calves and making hay, yet gentle when he welcomed us to Sunday school and turned the pages of his Bible.

I imagine your hands a little like his, Jesus—hands with nicks and scars suggesting someone who grew up doing manual labor. Hands that speak of life and love. Your hands lift our faces to see the birds, that we might know the grace of God's boundless love. They bless children and heal broken bodies. Your hands reach out to touch the wounded places we hide from the world.

Every scar, line, and crease wears the love you have poured out on human frailty and aching need. So it pains the heart to see your hands in shackles. *Let him go*, the heart cries. *We need those hands. We crave their touch.* But no, those hands go, shackled, to do one last deed of mercy, one final act of healing love for every wound ever suffered.

Prayer

Touch every suffering soul and troubled place, Lord Jesus, with the hands of your healing love. Amen.

Mark 14:55-56, 61-64

Now the chief priests and the whole council were looking for testimony against Jesus to put him to death; but they found none. For many gave false testimony against him, and their testimony did not agree.... But [Jesus] was silent and did not answer. Again the high priest asked him, "Are you the Messiah, the Son of the Blessed One?" Jesus said, "I am...." Then the high priest tore his clothes and said, "Why do we still need witnesses? You have heard his blasphemy!"

To ponder

We need to look at Jesus until we can look out at the world with his kind of eyes. The world no longer trusts Christians who "love

Jesus" but do not seem to love anything else.—Richard Rohr, *The Universal Christ*

Silent knowing

No one has ever seen God. The Bible tells us that. But Jesus' eyes draw us into the one who knows us whole. Steady, calm, unwavering, his gaze penetrates to the core of our being, inviting us to rest, content just to be with him in silent knowing—two, yet one, joined in mutual love.

Such is the heart I feel in you, Jesus, as you stand before the council. Unruly passions of fear and hatred agitate their hearts, eager as they are to pounce and condemn. But not you; your heart is quiet and sure. You know who you are and what you will do, for your eyes are fixed on the one who calls you to this moment. And now you invite us into your gaze, that we may know what you know—this great Loving Mystery whom no eye has ever seen.

So . . . don't say a word. Just look into his eyes. There is no shame under his gaze, no condemnation, just knowing love, eternal and unwavering, inviting us home. Lose yourself in his eyes. You will see as you are seen.

Prayer

Let me lose myself in your eyes, Lord Jesus, that I may know as you know and see as you see. Amen.

March 30

Mark 15:1-2, 6, 8

The chief priests held a consultation with the elders and scribes and the whole council. They bound Jesus, led him away, and handed him over to Pilate. Pilate asked him, "Are you the King of the Jews?" He answered him, "You say so." . . . Now at the festival [Pilate] used to release a prisoner for them, anyone for whom they asked. . . . So the crowd came and began to ask Pilate to do for them according to his custom.

To ponder

Jesus, the Good Shepherd . . . lays down his life for his people. Some live this calling literally, shedding their blood as martyrs.

Others live it in the unstinting giving of their time, their energy, their very selves to those they . . . serve.—Joseph Bernardin, *The Gift of Peace*

Eye-to-eye

I'm not sure who looks more sad or weary as Jesus stands eye-to-eye with Pilate, the Roman governor. History tells us Pilate was a cruel and obstinate ruler. But here, carved in stone, we see something else. His eyes and mouth droop, as if his duties have taken a terrible toll. Perhaps he is world-weary from the wretched business of dispatching defiant and delusional souls to a bloody end, all to keep order in a restive province. One almost feels sorry for him, trapped by responsibilities that kill the soul.

And there you stand, Jesus, bound and exhausted from a sleepless night and the trial before the council. Your eyes weary, resigned, knowing you will soon die for the mission you have lived. Sorrow weighs heavily on your heart, as you, like Pilate, bear the burden of what you must do—with one big difference. You give yourself for the sake of love for this crazy world, while Pilate does it for power. Ironic then that you win our hearts with a power beyond any Pilate could ever imagine. For there you are, weary eyes and all, loving this world to the very end.

Prayer

Help us to bear the weariness of loving, Lord Jesus, that we may follow where you lead. Amen.

March 31

Mark 15:9, 11-13

[Pilate] answered [the crowd], "Do you want me to release for you the King of the Jews?" . . . But the chief priests stirred up the crowd to have him release [the prisoner] Barabbas for them instead. Pilate spoke to them again, "Then what do you wish me to do with the man you call the King of the Jews?" They shouted back, "Crucify him!"

To ponder

We are all saved by grace and the utter freedom of God to love who and what God wills, without our tit-for-tat thinking getting in the way of God's absolute freedom to love. . . . God is nonviolent love, and this is the only hope for [our] world.

—Richard Rohr, *Eager to Love*

Scandalous patience

Alone you are, Jesus, as the crowd cries for blood. Alone too are any who love you amid the shouts. If any remained (perhaps the women), their hearts surely trembled as bloodlust swept across the rabble.

What is wrong with us, Lord? Why does hate come so easily? Did hating you release rage the crowd could not otherwise express? Did watching you suffer allay their pain and exorcise the bitterness of peasant life? Did losing themselves in cries of vengeance fill a need to feel powerful?

All of these poison our hearts. But amid human malignancy, we must not lose sight of you, Jesus. For you are the very image of God's own heart in this and every moment of your life. Cries of vengeance surround you, but you do not rail against the injustice of your condemnation or the brutality of bloodlust. You take it all in, refusing to pay back hatred with hatred. You drink the cup of bitterness, returning blessing for brutality. Such is the heart of God, the scandalous patience of a love that receives the worst thing ever—and turns it into the best.

Prayer

Grant us patience amid hardship, Lord Jesus, that we may reveal the beauty of your divine heart. Amen.

April 1 / Maundy Thursday

Mark 15:25, 33-34

It was nine o'clock in the morning when they crucified [Jesus]. . . .
When it was noon, darkness came over the whole land until three
in the afternoon. At three o'clock Jesus cried out with a loud voice,
"Eloi, Eloi, lema sabachthani?" which means, "My God, my God,
why have you forsaken me?"

To ponder

"Seeing" Jesus' suffering is a reminder that . . . we are accompanied
by a God who, even if he does not—for whatever mysterious
reason—take away our pain, understands it. . . . During times of

the worst anguish in my life it has been this prayer that has most consoled me: speaking with the Jesus who knows suffering.

—James Martin, *The Jesuit Guide to (Almost) Everything*

Hold me to it

Every cross in every land speaks. A black Jesus drew me into to a side chapel in the great Gothic cathedral in Barcelona, Spain. I almost walked by, but the sight of him on the cross would not let me. He was leprous and beaten, suffering the pains of death, as he hung before a half-dozen people praying among the spare wooden benches facing the crucifix.

I took my place among the benches and watched him. A great love for every suffering of every human soul whispered from the crucifix: *This love will never abandon you. This love will meet you everywhere you go. Look at me and know. There is no place this love will not go for you.* I sat and prayed— offering my unanswered questions, aching wounds, anxieties about the future, and my craving to feel God's love warming me through. When words were done, I walked to the back of the chapel, but still couldn't leave. Turning to the crucifix, I shook my finger at Jesus. "I'm holding you to this," I whispered. "I'm holding you to this."

It's okay, came the reply. *That's what I am here for. Hold me to it.*

Prayer

God of endless love, find us wherever we go, that we may know that your promise is true. Amen.

April 2 / Good Friday

Mark 15:37-39

Then Jesus gave a loud cry and breathed his last. And the curtain of the temple was torn in two, from top to bottom. Now when the centurion, who stood facing him, saw that in this way he breathed his last, he said, "Truly this man was God's Son!"

To ponder

The death of Jesus took away the veil that prevents us, the ordinary people, from seeing into the true "holy of holies," that is, the inner heart of God. . . . We can now see . . . the heart of a God whose love is faithful enough not to let us die . . . even when in ignorance and malice we go on killing God and each other.
—Ronald Rolheiser, "Bringing New Life"

My brother's voice

We come to this story every year, Jesus, and my heart fills with love for everything you are and everything you do. You are totally given to the Father's holy dream, a kingdom where everything is joined in a single heart of love for every soul and all creation. And there you are, dying, completely surrendered to God's loving purpose.

Even as you cry out in abandonment, you trust that God's unspeakable love will use this —even this—to shred the veil between heaven and earth and light our world with divine life and beauty. Truly you are God's Son, revealing the loving Father who holds us and every future we will ever know. *Trust this love*, you say, *and never surrender hope, no matter how dark the night or how painful the moment.*

History doesn't tell us what happened to the centurion who somehow felt the truth of your being in this your darkest hour. Strange—he came to this hour to kill you, Jesus, but hearing him, I recognize the voice of a brother.

Blessed are you, Lord Jesus. By your holy cross you redeem the world.

Prayer

Jesus, may your passion and death be our strength and life. Lift us into love for everything you are and all you do. Amen.

Mark 16:5-6, 8

As [the women] entered the tomb, they saw a young man, dressed in a white robe, sitting on the right side; and they were alarmed. But he said to them, "Do not be alarmed; you are looking for Jesus of Nazareth, who was crucified. He has been raised; he is not here...." So they went out and fled from the tomb, for terror and amazement had seized them; and they said nothing to anyone, for they were afraid.

To ponder

Seized by the Spirit of the resurrection, we get up out of our sadness and apathy.... An undreamed-of love for life awakens in us ... and our painful remembrances of death are healed. We

encounter life again like children, in eager expectancy.
—Jürgen Moltmann, *The Source of Life*

Saint Harper

Harper recently became my new Easter symbol, a butterfly and much more. Blonde, six years old, with a gap-toothed grin, she lies on a chalk drawing of a butterfly—blue, pink, and yellow. The drawing, six or seven feet wide, dwarfs her frame as she stretches out her arms as if these are her wings—they are yours and mine too, of course.

Losing myself in Harper's grin, I catch a glimpse of what God has in mind for us. Joy, for starters—joy that is the breath of the risen Christ animating our souls, lifting us above the struggles, hurts, and drab routines that drain vitality from our limbs. Yes, joy and the peace of knowing, as saints have told us, "all is well," for the Spirit of the Resurrected One floods our hearts so that our mortal flesh grows bold and our spirits take flight. Our hearts reach out to embrace life in all its beauty and banality, delight and disappointments, loving it all nonetheless with that love that knows no limits—the love God is.

This affirmation of life is the gift of this day for every day. I know. Saint Harper tells me so.

Prayer

God of life, breathe your abundant Spirit into our hearts, that we may live with joy, peace, and love beyond all fear. Amen.

Notes

Welcome: Tanzanian traditional; tr. Howard S. Olson, b. 1922, "Listen, God Is Calling/Neno lal Mungu," ELW 513, refrain, st. 1. Text © Lutheran Theological College, Makumira, Tanzania, admin. Augsburg Fortress. Reproduced by permission. **February 17:** Elizabeth Liebert, *The Way of Discernment: Spiritual Practices for Decision Making* (Louisville: Westminster John Knox, 2008), 33. **February 18:** *Evangelical Lutheran Worship,* Holy Baptism (Minneapolis: Augsburg Fortress, 2006), 231. **February 19:** Rachel Held Evans, "Named Beloved," The Work of the People, 1:24–1:41. Accessed at www.theworkofthe people.com/named-beloved. **February 20:** Nadia Bolz-Weber, *Shameless: A Sexual Reformation* (Colorado Springs: Convergent, 2019), 179, 181. **February 21:** Edward T. Chambers, with Michael A. Cowan, *Roots for Radicals: Organizing for Power, Action and Justice* (London; New York: Bloomsbury Academic, 2010), 22–23. **February 22:** Nadia Bolz-Weber, "Demon Possession and Why I Named My Depression Francis," *Patheos,* June 25, 2013. Accessed at www.patheos.com/blogs/nadiabolzweber /2013/06/demon-possession-and-why-i-named-my-depression-francis/. **February 23:** Greg Boyle, *Tattoos on the Heart: The Power of Boundless Compassion* (New York: Free Press, 2010), 75. **February 24:** Benjamin J. Dueholm, "Hearing the Truth," *Brutally Ordinary Things* blog, March 11, 2019. Accessed at https://bendueholm.com/2019/03/11/hearing-the-truth/. **February 25:** James Alison, "The Forgiving Victim," July 25, 2011. Accessed at www.youtube.com/watch?v=8GgM3IG_fwo. **February 26:** William J. Barber II, sermon at Disciples of Christ General Assembly, August 15, 2019. Accessed at www .youtube.com/watch?v=2AmzFbtxAGY. **February 27:** Vivek Murthy, "Dr. Vivek Murthy and Brené on Loneliness and Connection," *Unlocking Us with Brené Brown* podcast, April 21, 2020, 36:00. **February 28:** Ken Untener, "Prophets of a Future Not Our Own," excerpted from a homily drafted for Cardinal John Dearden, 1979. Accessed at www.usccb.org/prayer-and-worship/prayers-and-devotions/prayers/prophets-of-a-future-not-our-own.cfm. **March 1:** Frederic and Mary Ann Brussat, *Spiritual Rx: Prescriptions for Living a Meaningful Life* (New York: Hyperion, 2002), 268. **March 2:** Joan Chittister, *Wisdom Distilled from the Daily* (New York: Harper Collins, 1990), 126–129. **March 3:** Richard Wright, *12 Million Black Voices,* reprint ed. (New York: Basic, 2002), 99–100. **March 4:** Rachel Held Evans, *Inspired: Slaying Giants, Walking on Water, and Loving the Bible Again* (Nashville: Nelson, 2018), 157. **March 5:** Parker J. Palmer, *The Company of Strangers* (New York: Crossroad, 1981), 42. **March 6:** Colson Whitehead, *The Underground Railroad* (New York: Doubleday, 2016), 272. **March 7:** Dorothee Soelle and Luise Schottroff, *Jesus of Nazareth* (Louisville: Westminster John Knox, 2002) 64–65. **March 8:** Diana Butler Bass, *Christianity for the Rest of Us: How the Neighborhood Church Is Transforming the Faith* (New York: Harper Collins, 2006), 25. **March 9:** Cynthia L. Hale in *More Power in the Pulpit: How America's Most Effective Black Preachers Prepare Their Sermons,* Cleophus J. LaRue, ed. (Louisville: Westminster John Knox, 2009), 62. **March 10:** Dwight J. Zscheile, *The Agile Church: Spirit-Led Innovation in an Uncertain Age* (New York: Morehouse, 2014), 57. **March 11:** Douglas John Hall, *The Cross in Our Context: Jesus and the Suffering World* (Minneapolis: Fortress, 2003), 76–77. **March 12:** Barbara Brown Taylor, *Holy Envy: Finding God in the Faith of Others* (San Francisco: Harper One, 2019), 209. **March 13:** Marilynne Robinson, *Lila* (New York: Farrar, Straus and Giroux, 2014), 237. **March 14:** Hannah Shanks, *This Is My Body: Embracing the Messiness of Faith and Motherhood* (Nashville: Fresh Air, 2018), 123. **March 15:** Rachel Held Evans, *Inspired,* 220. **March 16:** Chimamanda Ngozi Adichie, *Purple Hibiscus* (Chapel Hill, NC: Algonquin, 2012), 269. **March 17:** Layton Williams, *Holy Disunity: How What Separates Us Can Save Us* (Louisville: Westminster John Knox, 2019), 47. **March 18:** Arianne Braithwaite Lehn, *Ash and Starlight: Prayers for the Chaos and Grace of Daily Life* (St. Louis: Chalice, 2019), 119. **March 19:** Rozella Haydée White, *Love Big: The Power of Revolutionary Relationships to Heal the World* (Minneapolis: Fortress, 2019), 49. **March 20:** Emmy Kegler, *One Coin Found: How God's Love Stretches to the Margins* (Minneapolis: Fortress, 2019), 28. **March 21:** Lenny Duncan, *Dear Church: A Love Letter from a Black Preacher to the Whitest Denomination in the U.S.* (Minneapolis: Fortress, 2019), 10. **March 22:** Karen Gonzalez, *The God Who Sees: Immigrants, the Bible, and the Journey to Belong* (Harrisonburg, VA: Herald, 2019), 146. **March 23:** Elizabeth A. Dreyer, *Passionate Spirituality: Hildegard of Bingen and Hadewijch of Brabant* (Mahwah, NJ: Paulist, 2005), 146. **March 24:** Mary Oliver, "When Death Comes," *New and Selected Poems* (Boston: Beacon, 1992), 10–11. **March 25:** Pope Francis, "Pope at Mass: Culture of Encounter Is the Foundation of Peace," Council of Centers on Jewish-Christian Relations, May 22, 2013. Accessed at https://ccjr.us /dialogika-resources/documents-and-statements/roman-catholic/francis/francis2013may22. Text from Vatican Radio. **March 26:** William A. Barry, *Paying Attention to God: Discernment in Prayer* (Notre Dame, IN: Ave Maria, 1990), 56, 58–59. **March 27:** Julian of Norwich, *Showings* (Mahwah, NJ: Paulist, 1978), 342. **March 28:** Henri J. M. Nouwen, *The Return of the Prodigal Son* (New York: Doubleday, 1992), 96. **March 29:** Richard Rohr, *The Universal Christ: How a Forgotten Reality Can Change Everything We See, Hope For, and Believe* (Colorado Springs: Convergent, 2019), 31. **March 30:** Joseph Bernardin, *The Gift of Peace* (Chicago: Loyola, 1997), 146. **March 31:** Richard Rohr, *Eager to Love: The Alternative Way of Francis of Assisi* (Cincinnati: Franciscan Media, 2014), 187, 189. **April 1:** James Martin, *The Jesuit Guide to (Almost) Everything: A Spirituality for Real Life* (New York: HarperOne, 2010), 298. **April 2:** Ronald Rolheiser, "Bringing New Life," *America,* October 5, 2015, 16. **April 3:** Jürgen Moltmann, *The Source of Life: The Holy Spirit and the Theology of Life* (Minneapolis: Fortress, 1997), 81.